Get Out of the City and Thrive!

Book 1: How I Did it and How You Can, Too!

By Robyn Dolan

ISBN-13:
978-1546747307

ISBN-10:
1546747303

DISCLAIMER

Thank you for purchasing "Get Out of the City and Thrive! Book 1 – How I Did it and How You Can, Too!" I hope you find it enjoyable, entertaining and helpful.

All persons in this book are real, though most of the names have been changed to protect the innocent (me). Some persons are composites of several different individuals, no likeness to one particular person is intended and composites are used merely for the author's convenience in illustrating a point. All information presented in this work is considered correct as of the time of its writing. All information is presented for educational and entertainment purposes only, no warranties are made and author assumes no responsibility or liability for misuse or misunderstanding of this information or damages due to use of information contained in this book.

This book details the author's personal experiences with and opinions about moving out of the city and making major life changes. The author is not licensed or certified to teach or give legal or medical advice. This book is not a substitute for legal, medical or accounting advice from a licensed professional.

This book provides content related to relocation, lifestyle changes and homesteading topics. As such, use of this book implies your acceptance of this disclaimer.

ROBYN DOLAN

DEDICATION

TO MY DAD, BOB SIEMANN. YOU WERE THE ANSWER TO A LITTLE GIRL'S PRAYERS, MY BIGGEST CHEERLEADER, AND MY SAFE HARBOR. I LOVE YOU ALWAYS.

ROBYN DOLAN

ACKNOWLEDGEMENTS

So many people help to write a book. First and foremost, thanks be to God, for the inspiration and constant unrest until I am doing what (I hope) He seems to want. To Yak, for putting up with mom's writing moods and learning curves. To Maryruth and Charles, for never letting up in encouraging me to write and plow into the book business. To my older children, for not putting me in the psych ward. Yet. To Jonah for, keeping me young. To my parents, for not being overly disappointed that I did not choose law or medicine as my vocation. To the folks at Grit Magazine, for letting me in as one of their reader bloggers back in 2008, and occasionally using my work in their publications.

Table of Contents

Stories My Dad Told
Me………………………………...……………..2

Making the
Decision…………………...……………………7

My Childhood
Dream………………………………………….9

Start With What You've
Got……………………………..…...……...12

Your
Job…………………..………………………15

Your
Financials………………………………......18

The
Kids…………………………………….......22

Your
Lifestyle……………...………………….......25

Getting Ready to
Go……………………………………….29

Mountain Real
Estate……………………………………31

Setting Financial Goals..34

Location, Location, Location...37

You Are What You Watch On TV.......................................38

Do Your Homework...41

Packing up and Moving out..43

Make an Action Plan..43

Time for a Change...44

Setting a Date...47

Sell or Give Away Your Stuff..50

Leaving Paradise...53

Settling Down and Settling in...56

A Family Adventure...58

Get Involved in Your Community...63

Conclusion...67

Resources for More Information...68

Websites...68

Books...76

You Tube...81

Can you Help me Please...82

About the Author...83

ROBYN DOLAN

GET OUT OF THE CITY AND THRIVE!

BOOK 1 – HOW I DID IT AND HOW YOU CAN, TOO!

"The year 1940 is still remembered in Minnesota as the year of the SNOW STORM. It was COOOOOLD. After the storm the snow was piled so high against our house that we sledded out of our upstairs window.."

STORIES MY DAD TOLD ME

From the time I was eight years old I can remember my dad telling me and mom and grandma stories around the dinner table about growing up on the farm. Getting up early to milk the cows and plow fields may not seem exciting to most kids and certainly dad was glad he didn't have to do that anymore, but to me there was a certain allure.

Dad was born in Downey, California. His parents, from Minnesota and South Dakota, wanted to raise their boys "back on the farm". So they moved back to a farm outside of the small town of New Munich, Minnesota. I will let dad continue the story from here:

"We boys were now expected to help with milking the cows, separating the cream and cleaning the barn. Jack, the youngest brother, milked old Rosie. She was a gentle, patient cow. Jack would take the milk pail and set it beneath Rosie, go get the stool to sit on while milking, then proceed to milk her.. She never once kicked the bucket or stepped in it or in any way disrupted the event.

On this farm we had an indoor toilet and bathtub; a novelty for farms in that part of the world. There was, of course, the two-holer also.

The year 1940 is still remembered in Minnesota as the year of the SNOW STORM. It was COOOOOLD. After the storm the snow was piled so high against our house that we sledded out of our upstairs window. The well and pump-house were next to the house; the cow yard with a water tank was about 25 feet downhill from there. There was a galvanized pipe from the well to the cow tank. My brothers and I discovered that we could make marks on the pipe with our tongue. As we continued doing this we finally got ourselves frozen to the pipe and couldn't get loose. Dad had to come with the teakettle and pour hot water on the pipe to get us loose. Lesson Learned!

We next moved to my maternal grandpa's farm. Back to square one regarding toilet accommodations; no bath tub, no indoor plumbing. There was a single accommodation building halfway between the house and the barn. No company welcome. There were, however, two major advances. We had electricity and we had a telephone.

Our chores now increased dramatically. We would get up every morning before daylight, pull on our work clothes and trudge to the barn, milk the cow, separate the cream, pitch hay to the horses and cow, empty buckets of slop into the pigs' troughs and feed scratch grains to the chickens. We would take special care of any particular animal we were raising to show at the fair or sell and then trudge back up to the house where mother was fixing a hearty breakfast. Then we would be off to school, walking the three miles to town in all kinds of weather, of course; pa would hitch up the team and go out and plow or plant the fields and repair fences and farm equipment. After school we fed the animals, chopped wood for the stoves, carried same to house, ate supper and milked the cows. The cow barn had a center aisle with stanchions along both sides. Each cow knew her proper stanchion. There was a gutter along both sides of the aisle into which the manure was scraped. When it became necessary, we cleaned these by loading the manure into the manure spreader; a wagon box with conveyor belt in the bottom and a spreader device attached to the rear. We used horses to pull this into the barn center aisle and, with one of us on one side and another on the other side, loaded the manure from the gutter into the spreader. When the barn was clean we hauled the manure to the field and spread it. This employment entailed sometimes getting splattered! The joys of farming! The Gieske farm was renowned for its rocks. Each spring, before planting, we had to "pick rocks". We had a "stone boat", a platform on the ground, which we drug with a tractor. It had to be on the ground so we wouldn't need to lift big rocks very high to load them. We had two big stone piles on to which we would dump our load. We found the rock pile a fine place to play!

I loved threshing time. One neighboring farmer owned the threshing rig, others hired him and his rig to thresh their grain. All who did so helped thresh wherever the rig went. It was a good time when all got together. Our job as "kids" was to man the spout through which the grain came out. We had to shovel the grain to the front of the grain wagon, fill the wagon, then take it to the granary and unload it; then get back to the rig and again fill it with the threshed grain. Once in a while we got to "spike pitch". That meant help load the bundles onto the bundle wagon. I really enjoyed spike pitching!

We raised chickens, hogs, sheep, and milk cows. One day I went out to the pasture to bring the cows up for milking. I rode one of the horses. As we were going along, a rabbit jumped out. The horse got into the game and really stretched out! As we neared a bush a second rabbit jumped out. The horse went after the second rabbit while I continued after the first. I landed in the bush, which was a tree stump with new shoots growing out of it. I landed on my back, on the stump! I lay stunned for a time. When I finally tried to get up, I couldn't. I thought I had broken my back. After several attempts and not being

4

able to get up, I got scared. No one knew I had gone out there. How long before they might find me? Finally I was able to roll onto my stomach, crawl to the fence, and pull myself up the fence to get on my feet. At first I couldn't pick up my right foot to walk, so I pulled myself along the fence, planning to do that until I reached the barnyard. As I went I found my foot was working so I was able to get home. I still have a bad back from that incident. I decided then that horses were for pulling wagons and plows, not riding!

Winters in Minnesota can be pretty rough! Often the road would be impassable by car because of the snow. It usually took a couple of days before the snowplow would get to our neck of the woods, so we'd have to get to town via the bobsled. A bobsled is one in which the front end is separate from the back, though hooked together by a pole. This allows turning like a wagon can. We put the grain box on the sled, loaded the cream, eggs and people; hitched up a team of horses, and off we went! 'Twas often bitterly cold! Shoveling snow was a major winter occupation.

Haying was always a fun time. We'd use "sling ropes" to get the hay into the barn. Most of the time we used horses but sometimes the tractor. First we laid a sling rope on the bottom of the hayrack, spread out enough to engulf the hay, then load hay until we figured it was right, then lay the second sling, load 'til again enough; lay the third sling and load until full. We would bring the load to the place where the hay door was, pull down the "carrier", attach the first sling, pull that into the barn and with the trip rope, drop the hay where we wanted it in the barn. Then repeat the process until done.

My Mother died in 1949. Dad decided to go to

California. First we went to South Dakota to visit his side of the family and we ended up staying two years. My cousin talked him into buying a farm which bordered on a game refuge. My cousin loved duck and goose hunting. Being right next to the reserve afforded an excellent location for hunting season. The farm was about three miles south of Hecla, Hecla being a few miles south of the North Dakota line. We were there about a year and a half. Crops failed and we were fortunate enough to sell the farm to an avid hunter who had money and dreams of building a hunting lodge. We now continued the original plan to go to California. Dad was re-employed at Rancho Los Amigos farm department; he had worked there some 16 years prior. I finished high school at Downey Union High School and was employed during the harvest season at Rancho. Rancho was perhaps the last place in the U.S.A. which still harvested with binder, thresher, and horse drawn bundle wagons. I shocked the grain. One day the boss came out and asked me if I could teach the young man with him to shock. He lasted about two after school evenings, then disappeared. Guess he didn't like the work."

Such was the stuff of our dinner conversation.

Making the Decision

I have tended to make major life changes without a lot of forethought or planning. This has its drawbacks, to be sure, but jumping in with both feet also has its advantages. One being that you don't wait a lifetime to do what you want to do, stuck in a job and a place that is terribly unsatisfying but for the paycheck. I'm not going to encourage anyone to compulsively quit their job, pack up the car and pitch a tent in the desert, but I will share my story, along with hindsight suggestions for improvement.

Making and implementing a plan before jumping in with both feet is a much better way to make a major life change. Either way, don't look back. Move forward. Mistakes can be remedied along the way. I know, I've made plenty of them.

"It was my childhood dream. A place in the country, with horses, pigs, chickens, fluffy rabbits, peaceful cows and a big, bountiful garden. "

MY CHILDHOOD DREAM

It was my childhood dream. A place in the country, with horses, pigs, chickens, fluffy rabbits, peaceful cows and a big, bountiful garden.

I envisioned green, rolling hills, neat, orderly pastures and plentiful grazing. My horse barn would be big enough for several horses, a milk cow and chickens, and the stalls were always clean. The pigs had their own little pasture and shelter. Every day I would ride my horse into the countryside, across the gently rolling hills, past ponds and streams, and in and out of shady woodlots. Sometimes I would ride up the dirt road and visit with neighbors or meet up with a friend who would ride with me.

There would be barn dances and picnics, quiltings and cannings. I had my community all dreamed up and ready to go. There were big Sunday dinners with Mom and Dad, who lived in their own little house nearby, and Victorian Christmases with every visible inch of house wreathed and garlanded and at the very least covered with a light dusting of snow.

There would be orchards of apples, pears, cherries and walnuts, blueberry bushes, and voluminous strawberry patches. Huge patches of sunflowers and peanuts; bursts of green lettuces, cabbages, peas and beans. There were tall stalks of sweet corn, orange pumpkins, green acorn squash, huge summer squash, tiny creamy patty pans, to supply my table, and plenty of fresh milk and eggs.

My children would come bounding off the school bus, eager for fresh baked cookies and steaming hot chocolate that would always be waiting for them on the kitchen table.

Then they would gleefully do their chores, clean out stalls, split and stack firewood, weed the garden and brush their horses, then take them for a nice little ride before supper.

I would arise early every morning for coffee and head out to the barn. I could feel the warmth of the cow as she stood perfectly still, patiently waiting for me to fill bucket after bucket of creamy, white milk. The barn was warm and sweet smelling and always full of plenty of hay and grain. After I milked the cow, the hens would practically hand me their fresh, warm, clean eggs and I would bring my bounty to the kitchen where it would magically transform itself into a hearty breakfast and ice cream, butter and cheese.

That was how I dreamed it. The reality turned out to be much different. But I'm not disappointed. In fact, I'm so happy to be living life in the country I might even be satisfied with a cardboard box. Until it rained. Or snowed. Okay, so I definitely appreciate my house. The point is, don't let ideals or perfectionism prevent you from taking steps to improve your life.

"Many people move out to the country to escape the rat race, only to recreate it again."

START WITH WHAT YOU'VE GOT

Take inventory of your present situation. Take a good look at your job and your financials. First look at them together, as in how much you're making and how much you're spending. Then include your spouse's income and expenditures. Look at what you're spending on necessities: food, shelter, clothing and transportation. Look at what you're spending on other stuff: entertainment, education, vacations, etc. How much is within your means and how much is going onto credit cards? Are you paying off your credit cards every month or carrying a balance and paying interest? Is this creating extra stress?

Before you throw out the whole idea, because you can't see any way out financially, also take a look at them separately, as in essentials and non-essentials. Or, if the zombie apocalypse happened today, what would you absolutely need to survive?

If it's just you, that makes it much easier. Getting spouse, ex-spouse (if minor children are involved), parents and grandparents on board with your decision can be very tricky. Teenagers are notorious for objecting to change. That was one of my mistakes! Having the support of parents, grandparents and children is very helpful. In the end, though, remember the primary decision makers are you and your spouse.

Throw out a conversation starter and see what kind of feedback you get. This will give you other perspectives to ponder and possibly influence your process. Also, try to do this before you've absolutely made up your mind with no turning back. Your family may strongly object to the idea at first, but once the seed is planted, and regularly returned to, even briefly, the desire may take hold and grow. Then you will start getting constructive feedback and food for thought. You might even get everyone on board with the plan.

At the end of the book I have included a number of websites, books and YouTube video links for further information on talking to your spouse, family and children about this important decision. Also for further advice and thoughts on job satisfaction, budgeting and lifestyle changes.

Why is it that you want to flee the city?
What is it about the rat race that you need to get away from?
How do you envision yourself living after you make the move?

These are important questions. Many people move out to the country to escape the rat race, only to recreate it again. This is not conducive to a happier, more sustainable lifestyle. So make a list of hard questions for you to answer. Maybe even bring a couple of friends or your family in on it. Others will come up with some very good questions. Right now, we want to find out why you want to do this. This will influence all your other decisions, including what you are going to do for a living, where you are going to live, how you are going to create your new life and when you are going to make the big move.

"Moving out of the city is not just for those who can work online. There are many jobs that can be had in rural and remote locations."

YOUR JOB

Are you happy with your present job and working conditions?

If so, will you be able to continue in your present job if you move out of the city?

If not, what is it that you are not happy with? Can it be fixed by a promotion, transfer or change of schedule?

Do you enjoy your work or just tolerate it for the paycheck?

If you enjoy your work, can you find the same kind of work where you are hoping to move to?

If not, have you been looking for other employment?

Do you have a long commute?

Could you move closer in? Can you find comparable employment closer to home?

Is manual labor taking its toll on you?

Do you have the skills to transition to a desk job or lower impact work?

Can you go back to school to get a degree, certification or skills that will enable you to get a job where you don't have to do manual labor?

Could you do your job remotely?

Is it a job that you could replace easily?

Do you do much of your work on computer, phone, or creatively?

Are you in the food service industry, construction business, or self-employed?

Are your skills in high demand?

Are you a nurse, computer programmer/troubleshooter, engineer?

Are you overly stressed or burned out?
Is your health suffering?
Do you feel closed in and need more space around you?
Is the traffic on your commute making you crazy and contributing to a rise in your blood pressure?

Moving out of the city is not just for those who can work online. There are many jobs that can be had in rural and remote locations. Some people choose to commute an hour or more for work, or stay in town for a few days a week while working. Many teachers, medical personnel and other professionals who make enough money, will rent a room or keep an apartment near work and just commute a couple of days a week.

Then there is consulting and sales work. Appointments can be made over the phone and grouped into a couple days a week, to cut down on commuting. Other jobs/businesses that can be worked closer to home might include: food service, medical clinic, convenience/grocery store; house cleaning, errand/grocery shopping service; home care/companion for elderly; child care.

There are many other ways to make a living in rural areas, but I will go into that in depth in Book 3 – Paying for the Dream – How to Thrive on Your Homestead. For now, you are evaluating your present situation.

"Putting in a few extra dollars over the minimum payment each month can make a big dent in the bill by the end of the year."

YOUR FINANCIALS

How much debt do you have?

Are you paying it off as quickly as you'd like?

Putting in a few extra dollars over the minimum payment each month can make a big dent in the bill by the end of the year.

How much are you actually spending on needs? (Shelter, food, transportation, clothing, utilities, medical care.)

Be careful in distinguishing needs from wants. Shelter is just that. It does not mean luxury (unless that is your priority). Food should be nutritious, but does not have to be expensive. You can cook at home rather than going out to eat. You get the picture.

How much are you spending on wants? (Entertainment, stuff, vacations, gadgets, toys.)

Do you really need that expensive satellite or cable tv package? How often do you really need to upgrade your phone? Have you checked other phone service plans lately?

What can you cut out of the budget and still be comfortable?

When is the last time you exercised your gym membership? Do you really need a gardener or can you mow the lawn yourself? Even better – take up part of that lawn and put in a vegetable garden.

What discomfort are you willing to adjust to in order to pay off your debt?

How about giving up sodas? Drinking water can become a good habit. A slice of lemon can improve the flavor. Put the extra couple bucks a week on that high interest credit card payment.

What are you willing to let go of to declutter your life and have more time with your loved ones?

The stuff in your storage unit, shed or attic is kind of obvious for yard sale inventory. What about the clutter in your living room? Do you really need to keep every single newspaper and piece of junk mail? If you've been saving plastic bottles for years and still haven't gotten to that make-a-boat-with-plastic-bottles project, it's time to let go. Sometimes, holding on to the recycles to cash in just isn't worth it. Put it in the trash.

What sacrifices are you willing to make to redesign your lifestyle?

Consider whether downsizing will help reduce your debt and your stress level. If you sold the house and got rid of the mortgage could you afford a smaller house that was paid off or had smaller payments? Could you stand to live in a smaller house?

If you have a car payment, would it help to sell or trade in the vehicle and get something with a smaller payment or pay cash for a gently used vehicle (keeping in mind you might be trading payments for repairs)? If you have more than one vehicle, can you make it with just one and get rid of the extra(s)?

Want to try to be a one car family? Try it out for a month. Work out your schedules and ride sharing before selling the second car. If you can do it for a month, then dump the excess weight.

Most spouses will agree that they would like to get out of debt. Start this conversation and see where it leads. If you find your spouse is unwilling to even consider any changes, make a few small ones yourself that will not affect their income or expenditures. Apply the money you've saved to paying off debt and then have the conversation again, illustrating how your own changes have affected the budget for the better. Small steps, over a long period of time may be needed here, and both of you may need to adjust expectations and desires before you come to an agreement about lifestyle change. When you're talking about your marriage, it's worth it to take your time with this.

There are hundreds of free and paid online resources for getting out of debt, managing finances and investing for the future. I have included just a few to start you off in the Resources section at the end of this book. There are even some budgeting worksheets available in the links provided.

The good news for singles, or marrieds who agree about making the change, is that now you can cut the fat, pay off debt, and make your move.

"Finding trustworthy child care is a challenge no matter where you live."

THE KIDS

If you have children there are some other considerations to deal with. Availability of activities and child care, schools or homeschooling, and living conditions. Adults can live in a tent with no running water and find solutions for hygiene and such. Children can certainly do this as well, especially on a camping trip. But when that camping trip stretches into months and years, you run the risk of social services finding out, and they tend to frown on raising children in such a non-traditional setting.

Of course, living in an rv or travel trailer can be a solution to this. Many families live this way for years, on purpose, and thrive. Depending on your rig, you can have water, power, heat, air conditioning, a large fridge, comfortable beds, satellite tv and even a washer and dryer! With solar panels, good batteries and a quiet generator, you could live for weeks at a time without even paying rent.

If you are working away from home, child care could be an issue. Finding trustworthy child care is a challenge no matter where you live. Check out the schools in each prospective location and ask about after school care and referrals.

If you are homeschooling you are in control of the quality of your child's education and you are more likely to be their primary caregiver. You may work at home and never need a babysitter, or you may work away from home and need trustworthy and reliable care. Ask at the local schools about after school programs and referrals for child care. No need to explain that you don't intend to enroll you child. Just explain that you are thinking about moving into the community and are checking out what is available for your child.

What activities are available for the children in the area you are moving to?

Is it a retirement community?

A college town?

Are there many other families in the area?

Are there community sports, arts and literary programs for the children?

Boys and Girls Clubs?

Scouting?

4H or Future Farmers of America?

You may not think you want to put your child in many activities, but when you slow down the pace of life, there are a lot of extra hours to fill, and you may need some options so they are not plopped in front of the tv or computer all day.

Of course, if you move out to the country and have a couple acres, you can always chase them outside to play for several hours. In some small towns, you can still see such nostalgic visions as children running around the yards playing freeze tag, riding bikes and skateboards, and playing basketball in driveways.

"When you live 50 or more miles from the nearest large town, it pays to learn to make a day of it once a month instead of constantly driving back and forth."

YOUR LIFESTYLE

Do you feel like you're a slave to your stuff instead of enjoying it?

Next time you're out shopping, pass up everything you don't absolutely need and see how long you can make do without it. You might find that you've been making quite a few unnecessary purchases.

Have you endured a death, divorce or other major life event that has left you feeling a great need to recreate yourself and your life?

Be careful here, but don't entirely discount the idea. I have found it very refreshing to reinvent myself from time to time. Especially when I have gotten myself stuck in a rut. That doesn't necessarily mean that you have to relocate and change jobs to do it. But sometimes it does.

Do you plan on growing a garden and having dairy animals and chickens?

Make sure you can do this where you plan on moving to. Some cities and counties have restrictions on where you can grow vegetables and other edibles; how many and what kind of livestock you can have – even out in the boondocks; whether you can butcher your own animals, and how to dispose of the carcass.

Want to rv full time?

If you don't already have your rig, better start looking around. You can find great used rigs for a fraction of the cost of new ones, but you will have to factor in repairs and maintenance. Even new rigs will have those considerations. Rent one for a couple weeks or months. Decide if you can even tolerate living in such a tiny space.

Just want a little house in a nice neighborhood, where you can walk to work and let the kids ride their bikes around the block?

Check out the job possibilities and get a few interviews; check out affordable housing and maybe try renting in the neighborhood for a couple of months, first. Nothing shows an area's true colors like living there for a while.

Do you need to be close to other family?

If you are helping out aging parents, disabled friends or relatives, or nieces and nephews, you may not want to move too far away. Look at other options to achieve your simpler life. Downsizing, gardening, taking more frequent day trips to the beach or vacations to the mountains may be a temporary solution. Or you may find that it's what you needed all along.

Is your extended family an important part of your social life?

Maybe you don't want to be more than a couple hours away. Check out the cost of living in less congested areas within your desired location. If you can't find anything affordable, keep working your way out until you do, then consider whether the distance is acceptable or if maybe what you really want is just a more affordable location within the city.

Consolidate your activities.

Start trying to grocery shop once or twice a month instead of every other day on the way home from work. Group and run errands all in one afternoon. Try and make medical or dental appointments for all family members at the same facility on the same day. Take in a movie or a show or have your dinner out on the way home. When you live 50 or more miles from the nearest large town, it pays to learn to make a day of it once a month instead of constantly driving back and forth.

As you examine and answer these and other questions that may come up, you may find that what you really need is not a whole life change, but maybe just a job change, a downsizing of your lifestyle, or more weekend outings. After making some of those changes, you may find yourself still dreaming about that place in the country. If so, move on to the next phase – Getting Ready to Go.

"I jumped into homesteading and just trusted that money and happiness would follow. It did. So did struggle, hardship and   sorrow."

GETTING READY TO GO

Some people like to have a plan for making a major life change. So do I. I just don't often have the patience to see the plan through. Sometimes I see it halfway through before I just jump in with both feet. I did not have the patience to finish college, to stick with a good job and make lots of money, to wait for retirement to pursue my other life dreams. I jumped into having children, to moving out of the city, to homesteading, and just trusted that money and happiness would follow. It did. So did struggle, hardship and sorrow. All of life, there for the living.

"We moved into a nice house about three blocks from my parents and started breeding cocker spaniels. It did not go well."

MOUNTAIN REAL ESTATE

I got married shortly after high school and gave birth to my first child, a boy, a year later. We moved into a nice house about three blocks from my parents and started breeding cocker spaniels. It did not go well. We had one successful litter, which we mostly gave away, and after two more unsuccessful tries, decided this was not a good idea. We had a large yard and I attempted a large garden in a corner of it near the avocado tree. Unfortunately, I did not have the funds to buy enough soil amendments, and was ignorant of composting, to make the gray alkaline soil productive. It did not help that I kept forgetting to water it. We did have a bumper crop of avocadoes, however.

My husband and I proceeded to get our Real Estate licenses. After a weekend ski trip to Big Bear Lake, a ski resort in Southern California, we decided to move there and shortly before our second child was born we did. In Big Bear I did not attempt any gardening. I was mostly concerned with making enough money to maintain and upgrade our lifestyle. We enjoyed skiing, playing on the lake and eating out. I also tried being a stay-at-home mom several times, but always ended up back in the office. We had always owned our own home since we got married. Towards the end, we also had a rental property.

When we divorced, we sold the properties, divesting ourselves of those encumbrances. I continued to sell real estate, in addition to managing rental properties, cleaning houses, and waiting tables at an upscale dinner house. After several years, it got to be too much. I no longer wanted to be the mildly successful real estate agent. I was sick of real estate. I wanted to get a steady paycheck and spend more time with my kids, who were growing entirely too fast. I needed to recreate myself. I wanted a new life in a new place where nobody knew me or had expectations based on what they thought they knew. A plan began to form. Big Bear was becoming an over populated, over developed city on a hill. Old pine forest was rapidly being replaced by subdivisions. Lake frontage was being swallowed up by mansions for the wealthy. The back country was being eroded by overuse from so many city folk coming up to play on the weekends. I was over extended physically, emotionally and financially. I had moved my real estate and property management office to my home, only going into the main office once or twice a week. I was waiting tables five nights a week and Sunday brunch. I was cleaning vacation and full time rental homes, and also doing yard cleanups. Something had to give. I saved up as much money as I could and went back to school for a semester to get my Emergency Medical Technician certificate. I figured I could work about 10 days a month and spend a lot more time with the kids. It didn't quite work out that way.

I got my Emergency Medical Technician Certification and started looking for work. The local hospital and ambulance service were fully staffed, so I had to commute off the mountain. Eventually the kids and I moved off the mountain. We found an apartment and later a house near my parents. I continued to drive ambulance and pay off my debts and save money towards the day I could move us out to the country.

"Nothing says "oops!" like running out of money 6 months into your new life."

SETTING FINANCIAL GOALS

This is important. Nothing says "oops!" like running out of money 6 months into your new life. Of course, if you're like me, you walk into the nearest likely dinner house and ask for a job. But even I had a financial plan to begin with. And the job was really a back up. In retrospect I should have done some better budgeting and avoided that altogether. Back to the financial goals. In the 2 years I spent back in the city, I rented from my parents and put every spare penny into savings or to pay off debt. At the end of the 2 years I was debt-free and had several thousand dollars in the bank. Enough to last us 6 months. I figured that was plenty of time to set up shop and get my businesses going (now I realize a year or 18 months would have been more realistic). In those 2 years, I also had a garden, ate lots of rice and beans, cooked from scratch and ate up the leftovers, and frequently ate at my parents' house. My 2 older children could babysit the younger one for a couple of hours if I was at work. If I was on a 24 hour shift, the kids stayed at my parents' house. Though my former babysitter was like family, and charged me practically nothing, with 3 children to be cared for, this still saved a huge chunk of the monthly budget.

Examine your budget. If you have debt, credit card or otherwise, take the loan with the highest interest rate and pay that off first. Maybe a 0% interest balance transfer would help. This depends on your individual integrity. Don't transfer your balance, then charge up the card again. Pay off loans from highest interest to lowest. Keep them paid off. When you get one loan paid off, put that payment amount towards the next bill and watch it pay down even faster. Then put that payment to the next one, and so on. Don't start your new life in debt. Unless you've already got a better job in your new location; just don't add any new debt.

Don't wait until the debt is paid off to bolster your savings. Even if it's only a few dollars a month, get in the habit of stashing some money in your savings account every month. If you have to, use the savings to pay lump sum bills like taxes and insurance, instead of putting these back on the credit cards. The goal is to keep saving every month.

Once all your debts are paid, put all the money you were paying them off with into savings and watch it grow by leaps and bounds. By this time, you have been doing some research and thinking about where you want to live, finding out how much it might cost, and looking for job possibilities in the area. Now it is time to draw up a rough outline of a budget and estimate how much you will need to get by for a year or so as you make the transition. If the number seems overwhelming, even with your new savings plan, set it aside for a few weeks, then come back to it. Re-evaluate wants and needs. Draft a realistic budget, and make a plan to achieve it. Maybe you need to stay put for an extra year. Maybe you need to downsize your plan. The big picture is not going to be affected by letting things percolate for another month or so.

Another thought on finances. Even if you have an 18 month cushion to start out with, it might be a good idea to have some potential jobs lined up or to get your business up and running, producing an income before you head out. There are a lot of adjustments to moving to a new location, and having the financial pressure off really helps.

Many good resources exist online for planning and sticking to a budget, getting out of debt, and investing. I have included a few at the back of this book in the Resources section to get you started.

"Location, Location, Location"

You Are What You Watch On TV

I was about nine or ten years old when I started reading the "Little House" books by Laura Ingalls Wilder. Then the books inspired a television series of the same name, which ran for a number of years. I rarely missed an episode. Those shows seem corny to me now, and the costume designers were certainly not meticulous or accurate. But the nostalgia and wholesomeness still appeal to me. The Daniel Boone television series and the Wonderful World of Disney, which often featured historical renditions, also figured prominently in my childhood entertainment.

The Little House books chronicle the life of a pioneer family in the late 1800's and early 1900's as seen through the eyes of their second eldest daughter, Laura Ingalls, later Laura Wilder. The family starts out in the "Little House in the Big Woods" of Wisconsin and from there, heads west as far as Kansas, where they find out, to their disappointment, that their homestead claim lies in Indian Territory. They must abandon their claim and head back east to Minnesota. The family travels by mule and ox teams, pulling their covered wagon; has several homesteads with varying degrees of success; battles Indians, wildcats and other predators, and somehow manages to survive. They build a sod house in the side of a hill on one of their homesteads. Later they put up a log cabin, just one room and the famous loft that the girls sleep in on the television series "Little House on the Prairie". Prairie fires and locusts destroy their crops and Pa takes on various odd jobs to make ends meet in between harvests. Ma somehow always manages to keep her chickens laying year-round and barters eggs for necessities from the general store. The storekeepers' children snub Laura and her sister Mary as "country girls". During a particularly severe winter, the family moves into town and Laura takes work as a seamstress. She also works on getting her teaching certificate, and meets her future husband, Almanzo. Laura and Almanzo marry and head west again, finally ending up in the Missouri Ozarks, where they continue to operate a small farm and apple orchard and Laura writes a popular newspaper column before penning her famous books.

Daniel Boone, in the television series, was portrayed as a rough, tough, yet gentle and sensible man. He brought his family to Kentucky and built a log cabin for them to live in. Then there followed more settlers and a log fort. The television show barely shows the hardships of pioneer life, focusing on the glamorizing of Boone's many negotiations to keep peace with the Indians. Daniel is often shown chopping wood, or bringing home a deer he's hunted. Rebecca, his wife is shown, sleeves rolled up, doing any one of the many "women's" chores, laundry, baking, sewing, scrubbing, and nary a hair out of place. And she always has a kettle of water hot and ready for tea.

In reality, as civilization moved in, Boone moved farther and farther out into the wilderness, sometimes to his family's dismay.

"There are many questions you will want answered before you find yourself stuck in a location you thought was ideal, then found out it is your greatest nightmare."

Do Your Homework

Even after researching all you can on the internet about your proposed new location, it is always a good idea to go spend some time there. This is where it can help to go full time in an rv for awhile. Or just rent a place for a month or so. Check out local campgrounds and rv parks, or use AirBnB or HomeAway to find possible rentals. Many local agencies will want a 6 month lease. You may only need a month or three to check the place out and decide to move on. Housesitting is another option. Check out the Resources section at the back of this book for links to get you started.

You need to check out the community you will be a part of. Make sure you are okay with the drawbacks.

Is it okay that the nearest decent shopping is 30 (or more) miles away?

Practice keeping a shopping list and shopping only once a month (or every 2 weeks) instead of running to the store every time you run out of something. Same with supply runs for repairs and such. Treat yourself to dinner out and a movie after your big shopping and supply run, and get a taste of what it will be like to be so far removed from conveniences.

Are there any organizations that you would like to participate in?

Living in the middle of nowhere may seem like a romantic notion to begin with, but boredom and loneliness do set in eventually. You may want other options for interacting with other people besides the local bar. Don't worry, there's always a local bar.

Are the schools acceptable?

Unless you plan to or are already homeschooling, you will want to check out the local schools. Just because they are in the "top 10 in the state", does not mean they are going to provide your children with the education you desire for them. Top 10 of what? Do so many of the children qualify for free lunch that the whole school gets it? This may sound good, but in reality, the government provided lunches are far inferior to those planned and prepared by real cooks, in those schools that don't qualify for school-wide free lunch. And in free lunch schools, children are not usually allowed to bring their own food from home.

If you are homeschooling are there resources available?

If you are not yet homeschooling, this may sound like a contradiction in terms. Yes, many homeschoolers buy their curriculum from homeschool suppliers or design their own. In fact, most homeschoolers are insatiable learners who require well-stocked libraries, arts and science programs, and yes, even sports.

There are many questions you will want answered before you find yourself stuck in a location you thought was ideal, then found out it is your greatest nightmare. Beyond just cheap land, fewer building restrictions, and a lower cost of living, you will, from time to time want the company of others, and some entertainment. Self-sufficiency does not mean isolation.

Packing up and Moving out

Make an Action Plan

Let's say you are single, or you have all your people on board with your desire to escape the city. Now it's time to make an action plan. This will involve setting financial goals, doing homework on location, jobs and schools, churches or other important ingredients of your lifestyle, and most importantly, setting a date.

Time For A Change

My close friends were all moving away. One to Minnesota, One to Northern California, two to Texas, one to Arizona. I was really itching to do the same. My friends in Texas enthusiastically encouraged me to join them. I was scared. I'd lived in Southern California nearly all my life, mostly with my parents in the same house, the rest in Big Bear. It was frightening to try to decide where to go and what to do. And if I didn't get it right, I might not have the money to get back to where I felt safe. Was I ready for adventure? Was I willing to take the risk?

When I landed a job running 911 calls near where my parents lived, we moved. I closed the rental business and quit my other jobs. Grandma and grandpa could provide child care while I worked. Now that I had full medical coverage, I got us all up to date on our shots, dental work, and vision care. Family support and help with the kids would free my overstressed mind to better make the decision that would change our lives. While we were at my parents' for Thanksgiving in 1996 I found a cozy little two bedroom apartment about two blocks away. It reminded me of one my grandma had lived in for a short time before she moved back into my parents' house. I signed a lease, paid a deposit and informed my children, who were overjoyed to live by grandma and grandpa. I explained to my parents that this would just be for a couple of years, until we decided where to move to and prepared ourselves. They were very supportive, but not very enthusiastic; but they were also overjoyed that we would be nearby. Especially my grandma, who was nearing eighty and could never understand why I moved away in the first place. I feel blessed to have spent extra time with my grandma before she died. She had always lived with mom and dad, in my memory, and was called to her eternal reward about a year after we moved back near them.

My oldest son played football and my youngest attended the school right up the street where my cousin was a teacher. We were a block from the church, close enough to walk. It seems like it should have been ideal. The pollution contributed to respiratory problems for all of us. I just could not resign myself to staying in the city. It was also very expensive. And my job was not allowing me to spend enough time with the kids.

I longed for the dark, starry skies of the mountains, a lake to play in and woods to hike in. I needed to figure out where to move to and then get started getting ready to do it. Ideas swirled around in my head. From just packing up the truck with the kids and dogs and driving until we decided to stop, to making a planned move and starting all over in real estate in a new place. Both options had their drawbacks, and I didn't really see a solution, but the desire kept growing.

At this moment I committed myself to changing my life and so began to save money and prepare for the next great adventure.

"Give yourself a deadline. This will give you the push you need to investigate your options for your new life."

Setting a Date

Give yourself a deadline. Set a date (you can always reevaluate and change it later) to make your move. This will give you the push you need to investigate your options for your new life.

Where do you want to live?
Do you envision yourself way out in the boondocks, off the grid, surrounded by trees or miles of desert?
Or would a tiny, quiet neighborhood in a small town be your ideal?
Maybe just a couple of acres where you could have a milk cow, some chickens and a horse?

How you will make an income once there?
Will you continue in your present job?
Work from home, telecommute, start your own business?
Is it practical to commute to the nearest city for work?

Do you want animals, a garden, homeschooling, good schools, a good size city nearby, medical care, etc.
Do zoning laws in your prospective area allow farm animals? If so, do they specifically forbid any particular animal or limit the number of animals?
Are vegetable gardens regulated or prohibited?
Is the local school district known for hassling homeschoolers or are they homeschool friendly/neutral?
If you will be using public schools, what is their reputation? Can you sit in on a few classes to check them out?
Do you have any medical conditions that need to be monitored regularly? Do you need easy access to medical care?

This will also give you some time to make a couple of visits to your desired area to see if it will actually work out for you. Once you have chosen your location and have a general idea of how you will make a living and what kind of lifestyle you are aiming for, re-evaluate your time frame and see if you need a couple more months or years. By this time, your deadline should be more realistic and you should be able to work seriously to achieve it.

"Moving is a lot of work and a lot of stress. The more stuff you have to deal with the more work, stress, and time it is going to take and the more distracted you will be from your ultimate goal."

Sell or Give Away Your Stuff

Moving is a lot of work and a lot of stress. The more stuff you have to deal with and keep track of (or store), the more work, stress, and time, it is going to take and the more distracted you will be from your ultimate goal.

As you start packing, ask yourself these questions:
Have I used it in the last year?
How many of these do I have/need?
Do I really need it?
Could it be a blessing to someone else?
Do I want to haul this around?
Do I want to pay for storage on this?
Do I really love it?

Especially with clothes, if you haven't worn it in the last year and don't really love it, maybe you don't really need it. If a sentimental item could really bless someone else, it is easier to let go of. Give it to that person. How many kitchen gadgets, sets of dishes and utensils do you actually use? Get rid of the excess.

Storing furniture and other large items or hauling them around with you might be more hassle and expense than hitting the thrift stores for replacements when you finally set up camp.

Make an offer or put a security deposit on your proposed property.

Having a valuable consideration vested in your enterprise will light a fire under you to get going. Just don't do this frivolously. A security deposit is just that – security that you are fully intending to follow through on your offer (also called earnest money).

Start packing.

Do not give notice at your job until you are locked into the move. Oftentimes employers will let you go "early" once you give your notice. You will want to be prepared for this misfortune if necessary. Having emphasized the need for caution and careful planning, don't let fear stop you from taking the leap. Just don't let overconfidence make you foolhardy.

Though this is the most important part of your action plan, giving yourself a deadline to do it, the date cannot just be set arbitrarily. You can start with a vague deadline of, say 2 years, but after doing some financial planning and location scouting, you will need to actually give yourself a real date on the calendar to embark upon your new life. This is because there are many preparations to be made, and you need the impetus to get going. This is not to say that the day cannot be moved forward or back. Just make sure you get going as close to your actual goal as possible.

"This is where it got interesting. Just as we got settled into our new routine, I noticed a disturbing fact. Every day at about 2:30p.m., the scent of marijuana would drift into our apartment. I could only guess that it was coming from the apartment next door."

Leaving Paradise

When I decided to leave Big Bear, the tiny mountain town in Southern California where I spent 12 years and gave birth to two of my four children, I moved quickly. I already had a job "down below" and was tired of the commute. Though I didn't really want to move back to the city, I had a much larger goal of moving out to the country in 2 more years. So I found an apartment across the street from my parents' home, packed up our stuff and started moving it into storage near the apartment, then packed up the kids and moved.

This is where it got interesting. Just as we got settled into our new routine, schools, job, time with grandparents, and writing time, I noticed a disturbing fact. Every day at about 2:30p.m., the scent of marijuana would drift into our apartment. I could only guess that it was coming from the apartment next door. The kids were not home from school yet, but the smell made me sick and I became very disappointed with the situation. I began looking for a cheap, bank repossessed house that I might be able to afford, and found one. As I was discussing with my parents whether or not to put a bid in on it, my mom, with her eye for a deal, found a much better located property that I could not afford. My parents, however, were looking for another rental and agreed to the amount that I would be able to pay. So they bought the house and we moved into it. It was about 3 blocks away from them, but closer to my youngest son's school, where incidentally, my cousin was a teacher.

As the time for our next move drew nearer, I made use of the newly affordable, dial-up internet connection and investigated property values in the areas I was considering,

Northern California and Arizona. I decided that our best option would be to start out in a travel trailer or rv, so that we could better check out the areas (the pot smoking apartment still fresh in my mind) and get my new Avon, Pampered Chef and Dorling Kindersley direct sales businesses going. (I was trying to cover all the bases). The critical factor in deciding between locations was my parents. I liked visiting them. The kids loved visiting them. I wanted to be available to them as they aged and I was keeping in mind the eventuality of having to move in with them for some years as they grew old. So I chose the location in Arizona 400 miles away, rather than the Northern California location 800 miles away. In terms of time and finances, Arizona just made more sense.

"We had sold our properties after the divorce, in a down market, for a loss, but that also meant that I did not have that encumbrance. "

Settling Down and Settling in

My hours as an Emergency Medical Technician were taking a toll on me.   I loved the work and only worked three or four days a week, but I was so tired from the twenty-four hour shifts that on my days off I wasn't spending very good time with the kids.

The money was steady though, and enabled me to pay off all my bills and save up about $3,000.

We had sold our properties after the divorce, in a down market, for a loss, but that also meant that I did not have that encumbrance.

Once I was no longer paying rent, I figured our expenses at about $500 a month, living in the camper. That would give us six months to find somewhere to live and build a home-based business in a new town.

"We dubbed our gypsy wagon "The Ark", and proceeded precariously down the road to the tunes of the major motion picture out the year before – "Titanic"."

A Family Adventure

When I moved to Arizona, I followed most of the plan. I paid off my debts, saved up some money and fixed up a place for us to live. I found an oversize cab over camper in the Pennysaver for $400 and did a little rehab on it. The corner jacks needed reinforcing. I put two coats of elastomeric on the roof after sealing the cracks with silicone caulk. I replaced the running lights and taillights and wired it to plug into the truck. I installed a support post on a cabinet above the kitchen counter. I put an old futon mattress I had been sleeping on in our rented home, on the bunk. I never got the toilet working, but we just used a gallon jug of water to flush. I also did not replace the water pump. We used a five gallon jug with a spigot in the kitchen and a gallon jug in the bathroom when we were not hooked up to pressurized water. I washed everything down with bleach water, especially the refrigerator. We heated hot water on the range. We got a small television with a built in VCR for movies, as we never really put a high priority on TV. Well, I didn't, anyway. I had a microwave-convection oven that took up almost the whole vanity counter. We crammed the wheel wells with firewood. Then we packed ourselves in. We were one adult, three children, a hamster, two dogs, a cat, our clothes, food and entertainments. We dubbed our gypsy wagon "The Ark", and proceeded precariously down the road to the tunes of the major motion picture out the year before – "Titanic".

Our destination was the home of close friends who had moved to Dallas, Texas a few years before. But we were in no hurry to get there. We toured Arizona and New Mexico, visiting the North Rim of the Grand Canyon, Roswell, Gila Cliff Dwellings, Smoky Bear's birthplace and Billy the Kid's resting place. Heavy winds caused the camper to sway precariously. When we got into Texas, it started raining. I searched the endless plains for signs of funnel clouds descending from the darkened sky and was never quite relieved until we reached The Alamo and the skies cleared. I never let the kids ride in the camper while we were driving for fear it would blow off the truck in spite of the heavy chains holding it down. The Titanic soundtrack was banished to a storage box for the rest of the trip. When we arrived in Dallas, it was the hottest, most humid time of the year. We thoroughly enjoyed our time with old friends, but I was disappointed with the weather, the city and the water. At any rate, despite our lovely friends, I crossed Texas off our list of options for relocation.

After we returned from our epic vacation, I went back to work for a few weeks. I put in a month's notice and we started packing. In my mind there were two remaining options – Northern California had always enchanted me. I also had friends and family there whom I hoped I could lean on as we adjusted. I loved the big trees, the ocean, the proximity to Yosemite and my other favorite national parks and forests. I poured over maps showing streams and lakes and imagined an ideal life in the woods and mountains, but near enough to the ocean to make a day trip once in awhile. With the wonder of the internet, I began investigating land prices and employment/small business possibilities. The expense seemed overwhelming but not enough to completely discourage me. In the end, I think it was the tendency of California to over regulate everything and the 800+ mile distance from my parents that led me to choose option 2.

Northern Arizona, near Flagstaff, had lots of affordable land, low taxes and fewer regulations. With the Grand Canyon nearby, there would be lots of seasonal work available, as well as my fallbacks of foodservice, hospitality and medical industries. It was also about 400 miles closer to mom and dad and I wanted to stay near to them as they got older, to be available to care for them. Arizona won out. Perhaps it was not the ideal choice, a bit drier than I liked, and not as many trees as I was used to. Also less snow and hotter summers. Fewer lakes and streams. But it fit into my tiny budget, and I would always be able to find work in the resort towns of Williams, Flagstaff or Tusayan. With the lower land prices, perhaps we could find some acreage to keep horses and other farm animals on. And a great, big, abundant garden. Maybe at some point it would be time to move on, but at least it was a start.

I relearned how to live frugally and do many repairs myself. I had a plan for making an income, even if it was a shaky one. I took a big breath and told myself I had confidence. Then I took a running start and jumped.

Back in California, we had a big yard sale and got everything down to one little storage unit. I read a pile of books about self-sufficiency and frugality (living as inexpensively as possible). I bought a fifty pound bag of rice, a fifty pound bag of beans and a fifty pound bag of popcorn. We had had a bumper crop of tomatoes from our garden and I canned enough red and green tomato sauce to last us a year. We would not starve. We packed up the camper with the least amount of stuff we would need to get by with one adult, three growing children, 1 dog, 1 cat and a hamster and headed east to Arizona, where it was hot and dry, and the land was cheap.

First we camped in Flagstaff for a few nights, but the price was high and so was the price of property we looked at. We migrated west to Parks and stayed in the most wonderful RV Park. We were surrounded by tall pines and set away from the street. The outdoor sinks were ideally suited to washing dishes, the bathrooms were clean and the showers hot. We set up a supply tent, to make more living space in the camper – if that's possible. The laundry room was a nice place to sit and read while waiting on the clothes. The kids were always in eye or earshot. The park was not overcrowded, especially that time of year, autumn going into winter. It was almost my ideal place to live, except that property in Parks was just as expensive as property in Flagstaff. The hookups were perfect for our setup, and the little market next door also rented videos. It really felt like home. I think we would have happily stayed there indefinitely, but when it started to snow, I panicked and we once again headed west to Williams. There we checked into a cheap motel for about a month until I lease-optioned a house. The more I looked around that house, the more I realized that it wouldn't do. The water heater was falling through the floor. The yard was too small for the horse I dreamed of getting some day for my daughter. We went west again to Ash Fork, looking for property.

More on our final homestead in Book 2 – Milking the Wild Goat – How to set up Your Homestead.

"I am one to whom the ideal of being isolated in the middle of nowhere sounds wonderful. But in reality, I do need the companionship and stimulation of other people on a regular basis."

Get Involved in Your Community

I am one to whom the ideal of being isolated in the middle of nowhere sounds wonderful. But in reality, I do need the companionship and stimulation of other people on a regular basis.

Go to church

If you embrace a particular religious faith, make sure there is a place of worship for that faith nearby. Getting involved in your church community can make a big difference in feeling at home, especially if you don't know anyone when you first get there. You don't have to "live" at the church, but offering up an hour or two a week outside of weekly services, or attending a class or bible study will help you meet people, learn about the area, and feel like you belong.

Be active in your community

Take a walk. Pick up trash. Deliver meals on wheels. Go to the local American Legion fish fry. Have lunch at the diner once or twice a week. Showing your face around town helps the locals get used to seeing you and opening up around you. Let them get to know you a little bit and you might pick up some tips about how people live and what they do in your new town. You might even *gasp* make some new friends who will help you settle in and feel at home.

Check out local clubs.

Um, I'm not talking about bars or night clubs, although if that's your thing… Most small towns have a library and/or community center. They can usually point you in the direction of clubs and activities held there and elsewhere in the community.

Libraries and community centers are always looking to get grant money, and usually need to provide some kind of proof that they need it. Special programs such as community classes, events, clubs, meetings, activities and participation in such help these facilities continue to get the grant monies they need to stay open for the community.

Start one of your own.

If you can't find any organization you're interested in joining, maybe you can start one. Ask the library or community center if you can teach a class, start a scrabble club or chess club, lead a yoga or zumba class or a weekly jam session for local musicians who may not have another outlet for performing.

Remember the magic of grant money. If you know how to write for a grant you have power. If not, you can learn. Most likely someone at the library is already experienced or at least trained to write for grants. Talk to the head librarian and to this person about your idea for a club or class.

Teaching a class may also be a way for you to pocket a little extra income, depending on your center's policies. More about this in Book 3 – Paying for the Dream – How to Thrive on Your Homestead.

Post a group on meetup, facebook, or a similar site, for hiking, photography or homeschooling.

You are not the only one looking for something to do and for a way to meet people. Thanks to the internet and social media, there are now lots more options to connect with like minded individuals.

Participate in local events.

Another great way to meet like minded people. I met my business partner when I attended an Art in the Park event. She was handing out cheese samples and we got to talking about uses for milk, cows vs. goats, making soap, and the conversation continues. I also discovered that not only one of the ladies I had met at church, but also our town librarian, are accomplished oil painters. My grandma had been an oil painter and I have a great admiration for art.

This is a good way to meet your neighbors and make new friends.

Lead a 4H group.

4H is not just about animals, if there are even a couple of kids interested, you could lead a sewing, cooking, gardening, forestry, or other group. If you are going to be working with minors, expect to have to endure a little bit of red tape. Keep in mind that background checks, fingerprinting, and detailed applications for these volunteer positions are intended to help protect minors from bad guys. If this offends you, don't expect parents to trust you with their children.

Take a class

Community colleges are also a good resource for learning to thrive in your new life. Many community colleges in rural areas offer classes in various methods of gardening, conservation, building, animal husbandry and other useful things. They are also a good way to meet other people in the area, if not specifically in your town.

Conclusion

Many people dream, at one time or another, of leaving the city and enjoying a "simpler" life in the country. Many of these never pursue that dream. If it is because of fear, set that aside. It is very doable. The process and timing are not the same for everyone who attempts this. But the basics are. Get the family on board, make a financial plan, start making the adjustments to your lifestyle and set a date. Investigate the areas you are interested in, ways to make a living in those areas and whether you can achieve the lifestyle you are aiming for there.

Then jump in. Do it. Don't look back. Keep moving forward, re-evaluating and living. Do not become a slave to your new life, that is why you're leaving the old one, right?

Live it, enjoy it, and thrive.

Resources for More Info

Websites: note – if link doesn't work, try to copy and paste into your address bar.

Deciding to move out of the city

Money Crashers – this article gives 14 common sense tips to help you when considering whether and where to relocate. The resources at the end of the article may or may not be helpful, depending on your situation. http://www.moneycrashers.com/where-should-i-live-decide-best-places/

Thought Catalog – another good article, separating the momentary desire for escape from the deep longing for solitude and simplicity. http://thoughtcatalog.com/carrie-a-laski/2014/06/should-you-move-out-of-the-city-a-guide/

To the Rural Life – start reading this blog here to find how one man made his decision to flee the city and how it all worked out for him. http://www.grit.com/community/from-the-city-to-the-country.aspx

Evaluating your job, finances, lifestyle

Dave Ramsey is the go-to guy for getting out of debt and wise budgeting and investing. Check out his tools page here for free helps with budgeting and more.
http://www.daveramsey.com/category/tools/?snid=tools

Forbes has a number of articles and tools to determine if you should be looking around for something better:
http://www.forbes.com/sites/lauragarnett/2015/01/30/quiz-is-your-job-right-for-you/

http://www.forbes.com/sites/dailymuse/2013/04/15/3-signs-you-should-definitely-quit-your-job/

http://www.forbes.com/sites/jacquelynsmith/2013/09/04/14-signs-its-time-to-leave-your-job/

In evaluating your lifestyle, take into account more than just happiness, activities, and stuff. Look at your job and finances hard and decide if maybe some of your lifestyle is just there to distract you from unpleasantness in the rest of your life. Refer to the articles above.

Zen Habits – a great website for thoughts on what is really important and how to simplify, minimize and streamline your lifestyle. http://zenhabits.net/start/

Grit Magazine reader blogs are chock full of info from country folk, farmers, urban homesteaders and the like. Here is the link to mine and from there you can browse dozens of others.
http://www.grit.com/blogs/homesteading-with-mrs-d.aspx

Lehman's Country Store has been supplying non-electric items to Amish and other families since 1955. Many of their products are Amish made. Most are made in the USA. Their blog is full of useful info about country life.
http://countrylife.lehmans.com/

Checking with the family

Kids Health has some good tips on helping children cope with moving.
http://kidshealth.org/parent/emotions/feelings/move.html#

Parent's Magazine has lots of useful articles on communicating with your children and helping them to adjust to major life changes.
http://www.parents.com/parenting/money/buy-a-house/make-moving-easier-on-you-and-your-kids/

Useful info for opening up the discussion with your

spouse. http://www.aliceboyes.com/relationships-communication/

Examining your motives

Some things to consider before you make the leap. http://www.blogher.com/five-things-not-do-when-you-are-making-really-big-change

Here is a good guideline for examining your motives: http://www.liveintentionally.org/2011/02/01/things-you-don%E2%80%99t-have-time-not-to-do-6-examine-your-motives/

Do you need a vacation or do you need a new life? http://www.theminimalistmom.com/2012/03/vacation/

Setting financial goals

Money Management International – budgeting tools, articles, goals worksheet. http://www.moneymanagement.org/Budgeting-Tools/Credit-Articles/Money-and-Budgeting/How-To-Set-and-Keep-Personal-Financial-Goals.aspx

Sorted – your independent money guide. Several articles about budgeting, financial goals, goals worksheet.
https://www.sorted.org.nz/a-z-guides/setting-goals

Smart About Money – several articles about financial goal setting. Goals worksheet.
http://www.smartaboutmoney.org/Tools-Resources/10-Basic-Steps/Set-Financial-Goals

Researching locations and jobs

Career Builder search by keywords for category, company, city, state.
http://www.careerbuilder.com/jobs/keyword/research

Many other job boards exist, including Craigs List and local papers which may be accessible online.

Wikipedia – put in the name of your prospective location. Be aware that wikipedia info is user-generated and may not be supported by other material.
https://en.wikipedia.org/wiki/Main_Page

United Country Real Estate specializes in rural properties, nationwide. You can get ideas of property values in your prospective location. http://www.unitedcountry.com

Google your prospective destination + real estate and see what comes up. Sites like Zillow and Trulia, as well as local real estate offices will also give you an idea of affordability.

Links that may help you find a place to rent for a few months while you're checking out your prospective location:

Airbnb.com

Homeaway.com

Vrbo.com

Flipkey.com

Depending on the owner, you may or may not be able to take your pets with you.

Housesitting

Housesitting is becoming a popular way to travel. Many owners are particularly looking for petsitters, so check the site out before you post your services. If you are allergic to dogs or cats, this may not be for you.

Rover.com

Trustedhousesitters.com

Luxuryhousesitting.com

Housesittersamerica.com

Minimizing and Relocating

21 Benefits of Owning Less
http://www.becomingminimalist.com/minimalism-benefits/

The Minimalists – a site entirely devoted to minimizing with lots of practical advice. Check out the archives for a complete list of articles. http://www.theminimalists.com/

Tiny House Blog – lots of articles about tiny houses and the tiny house lifestyle. http://tinyhouseblog.com/

Considerations when relocating:
https://www.mindtools.com/pages/article/considerations-when-relocating.htm

Relocation checklist: http://www.realsimple.com/home-organizing/organizing/moving/moving-checklist

Relocating without a job: http://career-advice.monster.com/job-search/getting-started/Relocation-Moving-Without-a-Job/article.aspx

Rving full time

Wheeling It – full time rvers since 2010, Nina and Paul are part of a growing community of younger full time rvers. Lots of info on real life situations on the road, as well as links to Paul's "Investing for a Living" blog. http://wheelingit.us/2011/09/22/10-things-i-wished-id-known-before-fulltime-rving/

Little House Living – the chronicle of one family's journey from 1200 square feet to full time rving. http://www.littlehouseliving.com/fulltime-rv-living

RV Road Trip: The Adventures of Jerry and Cynthia – Rving on a Budget http://rvroadtrip.us/library/fulltiming.php

Mrs. D's Homestead – my website and blog, where I write about our adventures from moving out of the city, to setting up and running our homestead, to transitioning to full-time rving/roadsteading. http://www.mrsdshomestead.com.

Homesteading With Mrs. D – my Grit Magazine reader blog. Here I post other items of interest about homesteading. http://www.grit.com/blogs/homesteading-with-mrs-d.aspx

Books:

All books available on Amazon as of date of this writing.

Deciding to move out of the city

Your Move to the Country, by Dennis Ogden An escape from the city.

Countryfied Chickens, by Chas Elliott A cautionary tale for anyone considering a move to the country.

From City to Country Living: A Guide to Those Making the Change by Arthur L. White, E. A. Sutherland How do we - people who have grown accustomed to city living, with all its conveniences - make the transition to country living?

Evaluating your job, finances, lifestyle

The Pathfinder: How to Choose or Change Your Career for a Lifetime of Satisfaction and Success, by Nicholas Lore

BOOK 1 – HOW I DID IT AND HOW YOU CAN, TOO!

_____ The Total Money Makeover: Classic Edition: A Proven Plan for Financial Fitness, by Dave Ramsey

_____ Off Balance: Getting Beyond the Work-Life Balance Myth to Personal and Professional Satisfaction, by Matthew Kelly

Checking with the family

_____ How To Talk To Your Kids & Grandkids: 10 Secrets To Being The Grandmother Everyone Adores, by Deborah Williams, Linda A. Johnson

_____ Communication in Marriage: How to Communicate with Your Spouse Without Fighting by Marcus Kusi, Ashley Kusi

_____ How to Talk So Teens Will Listen and Listen So Teens Will Talk, by Adele Faber, Elaine Mazlish

Examining your motives

WHY NOT?: The Question That Will Transform Your Life, by James Weaver

The Power of Habit: Why We Do What We Do in Life and Business, by Charles Duhigg

The Power of Positive Thinking: 10 Traits for Maximum Results, by Dr. Norman Vincent Peale

Setting financial goals

Budgeting: Personal Finance: Learn How To Manage Your Finances And Start Saving Now (Finance, Personal Finace, Self Help, Habit, Save Money, Goal Setting), by Dave Miller

Retirement: Early Retirement Success Secrets! - The Ultimate Retirement Planning Guide To Get Out Of Debt, Create Passive Income To Quit Your Day Job, ... Minimalist Budget, Organize Your Life), by Mick McPherson

The Minimalist Budget: A Practical Guide On How To Save Money, Spend Less And Live More With A Minimalist Lifestyle (minimalism, minimalist living, minimalist ... minimalism books, simple living, budget), by

Researching locations and jobs

Jobs: How to Find a Job in 30 Days, A Step by Step Guide (Jobs, Career Advice, Careers), by Henry Lee

How to Find Your Ideal Country Home: Ruralize Your Dreams, by Gene Gerue

Making Impossible Possible: How to Find and Create Your Dream Job, by Jon Lee

Relocating: How to Find the Best City to Call Home, by Claudia Rose

Minimizing and Relocating

The Joy of Less, A Minimalist Living Guide: How to Declutter, Organize, and Simplify Your Life, by Francine Jay

Do Less: A Minimalist Guide to a Simplified, Organized, and Happy Life, by Rachel Jonat

Moving Gracefully: A Guide to Relocating Yourself &
Your Family, by Carol Fradkin

Moving with Kids: 25 Ways to Ease Your Family's
Transition to a New Home, by Lori Collins Burgan

Rving full time

Complete Guide to Full-Time RVing: Life on the Open
Road, by Bill Moeller, Jan Moeller

RV LIFE- KEEP IT SIMPLE: From S&B to Mobile
RV...how to get there, one step at a time, by Beth Inman

RV Living For Beginners: Step-by-Step Guide To Start
Independent And Debt Free RV Living: (rv travel books,
how to live in a car, how to live in a car ... true, rv camping
secrets, rv camping tips,), by Roy Johnson

The Working Parent's Guide to Homeschooling: Tools
and Resources for Working Parents to Homeschool, by
Robyn Dolan

You tube channels of interest:

My Little Homestead -
https://www.youtube.com/watch?v=CuaodxQHf98
- Homesteading Setbacks | Country Living Adjustments

Appalacia's Homestead - https://youtu.be/9_wT3ltNeEI
Homesteading - The Dirty Truth

The Simple Life Home -
https://youtu.be/5Om6hwyhsM4 Homesteading - Is it
right for you?

Mrs. D's Homestead – my You Tube Channel
https://www.youtube.com/user/mrsdshomestead/videos

Can you Help me, Please?

I hope you have enjoyed *Get out of the City and Thrive - Book 1: How I did it and How You Can Too!* as much as I enjoyed writing it.

I would be so grateful if you would leave a review on my website at http://mrsdshomestead.com/site/shop/books-n-downloads/escape-the-city-and-thrive/

In return, if you will leave me your email address on any of my webpages in the newsletter sign up box, I will keep you updated about new book releases, free downloads, quick tips for homesteading, homeschooling and simple living and my latest blog posts, all in one weekly-or-so newsletter!

GET OUT OF THE CITY AND THRIVE!

BOOK 1 – HOW I DID IT AND HOW YOU CAN, TOO!

About the Author

Robyn Dolan escaped the city for the first time in 1986, as a young mother, with her second child on the way. The family moved to Big Bear Lake, CA and lived and sold Real Estate there among the tall pines, deep lake and hordes of skiers for 12 years.

After her divorce, Ms. Dolan decided to move even farther out and eventually settled in Ash Fork, Arizona, "50 miles from everywhere", west of Flagstaff and north of Prescott. Here she raised goats, sheep, chickens, horses, dogs, cats, the occasional pig, and a milk cow, for another 14 years. She also gave birth to her 4th child in Arizona.

GET OUT OF THE CITY AND THRIVE!

BOOK 1 – HOW I DID IT AND HOW YOU CAN, TOO!

Presently, the author is living full time in her 26 foot travel trailer, traveling between elderly grandpas and enjoying the sights in between. She calls her continuing attempts at homesteading and frugal living "roadsteading" and her son's homeschooling experience "roadschooling".